Musical Figures

poems

Samn Stockwell

Musical Figures

Copyright © 2023 Samn Stockwell

All rights reserved.

ISBN-13: 979-8-9861105-6-1

Cover art by Knox Peters

Cover design by Josh Dale

Printed in the U.S.A.

For more titles and inquiries, please visit:

www.thirtywestph.com

Advance Praise for *Musical Figures*

"In *Musical Figures*, Samn Stockwell's visions of a childhood enact a triumph over insufficiency and; pain — not by making claims for oneself but through the countervailing sounds of incisive remembrance."

—Ron Slate, author of *The Great Wave* and *The Incentive of the Maggot.*

"One could read the eponymous five 'musical figures' alone in this wondrous book and have a sense of a whole. But in so doing, readers would rob themselves of one moving moment after another. Like her figures, Samn Stockwell's poems might first appear as mere lists, but in a trice, they turn out brilliantly to render scenes and situations, physical, emotional, societal, and even historical. The reader is there in every sense. With a few exceptions, each work tends to be short, almost a supercharged haiku, that is. Stockwell is sui generis, no other poet I know delivers so much by way of such an artful economy."

—Sydney Lea, author of *What Shines* and former poet laureate of Vermont.

"Samn Stockwell's poems in *Musical Figures* are beautiful, searing, and intimate. Stockwell's sharply observed poems of domestic life explore emotional landscapes that expose what it means to be human. A magnificent achievement."

—Julie R. Enszer, editor and publisher of *Sinister Wisdom.*

"From the moment I heard 'the screen door opening and closing,' I knew I had entered a recognizable world; a world I would experience through touch and sounds. The poems in Samn Stockwell's *Musical Figures* are rich with the relics and detritus of a lifetime, 'a cradle, quilts, and a ukulele.' Tracing a lineage that includes the institutionalization of poverty, of mental illness, alcoholism, and war, Stockwell's speaker is 'busy fleeing my birth;/in a movie I would have shouted/don't go by yourself.' The poems refused to let me look away from 'the glue of everyday life,' this sticky trauma, this 'bowl of molasses kisses/wrapped in twists/of yellowed wax paper.' It is a close examination of humanity, where the speaker has 'other stories, who doesn't.' It's in this reaching out to the reader that Samn Stockwell opens their heart to 'making something,' to the constant and heart-breaking motion of "riding our bikes over the iron bridge/waving to our distant parents."

—Jennifer Martelli, author of *The Queen of Queens* and *My Tarantella*.

"In Samn Stockwell's collection, *Musical Figures*, moments of family history are relayed in crisp narratives fueled by lyricism. The combination of storytelling and musical phrasing result in poems both powerful and true. Above all, the voice is captivating: revealing everything in an understated manner, no matter the violence or catastrophe encountered, so that the reader leaves this hard-bitten, hardscrabble life with a sense of optimism and even well-being, as the speaker has remained calm, compassionate and credible, a survivor, and these are the hallmarks of her work."

—John Skoyles, author of *Driven* and *Yes and No*.

"Samn Stockwell's *Musical Figures* conjures past figures into the present and present figures into the past with a language of songs only Stockwell can create. These poems carry a voice that is hauntingly original, building a juxtaposition of the enduring beauty and pain of family and home through vignettes and surprising, sharp descriptions. This book explores a heritage of trauma, as time becomes nonlinear moving back and forth through the interactions of three generations. Stockwell shines a light on the why and how of a family who is injured and causes injuries with deft imagery that is both stark and beautiful, expertly evoking a combination of darkness and comfort — "through curls of cigarette smoke/cream streamed in our bowls." By focusing on one family, Stockwell offers a path for anyone to see and feel "the ways we infected / each other, here is a yellow / thumbnail much pried from the door."

—Natalie Padilla Young, author of *All of This Was Once Under Water*, managing editor of *Sugar House Review*.

For Cheryl

Contents

Musical Figures

Musical Figures 1

1. The screen door opening and closing
2. A cat in the wet field, curling his tail
3. A lunch box lid clanking on a school desk
4. A bell rings
5. The dog licks her paw in front of the gas stove
6. The father pulls down the hood of his car
7. A snake eats an egg
8. The bird quivers
9. The snake coils into cold sleep
10. Moths hitting the streetlight

For a Lost Ticket

I watch the moon flick
over orchard and fields
as I sift myself to sleep,
landing in a doorway of snow,
the sharp breath
of another century.

My parents are playing cards there,
homeless in the suburbs,
waiting for the conductor
to tell them to begin their lives.

And I chase them from station to station,
shaking their past before them.

Eulogy

I take the corpse of my mother out.
The ground is dry enough
for her to shuffle safely
across the parking lot.

She squints and admires the gulls,
if they are gulls.
I'll cry when she finishes
slurping out her rare words,
and some other her
can be summoned,
as partial, as extinguished.

My mother lived so long McDonald's died.

The five and dime migrated to the dollar store,
and the drugstore lunch counter
forever closed its gray Formica stall.

Tic

My mother shuddered, a two-step and a shimmy
a bug's crawling down my back

Before I was born, my mother was wrapped
in a covered tub in an asylum.
The women on the ward steamed in rows
my aunt among them.

I imagine my brother and sister
hauling my mother from the housing project
in their toy wagon
palms sweaty with the smell of the metal handle,
dragging the cart to the steep steps.

Antiques

My parents rifled houses left adrift.

I picked a pair of glasses
from a nest of bills.
My mother shuffled tintypes
of horses and hayfields.

As she stole, my mother inventoried
her childhood; paper dolls made
from catalogs, butter spread
on hot biscuits.

But the doll in the attic,
one wax eye tracking,
pursued my mother through the house
as my father's baritone bloomed
near the orchard, as he packed the car:
a cradle, quilts, and a ukulele.

43 Howland Street

When my father waved goodbye
sobs bent him bowed over his cane
while the car of his children disappeared.
Terrible fear is love
with its constant emptying
of assurances.

Long ago, walking in the early morning in Belgium,
his pack chafing his shoulders, his rifle jostling,
he couldn't see the next stretch, quiet
except for the feet of his platoon pattering,
and the sleepiest river gliding over its worn bed
he thought he had lost the weight of himself.

The Sale

My father bought a hearse for the family car
& severed his tendons putting in windows,
blood flooding the towel
on the drive to the hospital.
When he sold it, he patched the gas tank
to get the new owner home.
My father laughed, folding the check in his wallet.
My mother objected & they divorced
between children, a semicolon between clauses.
On the playground we milled in the cold,
currents of girls & a classmate said we couldn't be
friends:
your parents and she grimaced.

Sunday, Devon

As my family walked to church
my younger sister jumped
into the road and a Ford
leapt into her side.

When the driver emerged,
my father unfurled his arms,
leaping to the man's lapels
and tossing him to the ground.

My father was softly pinched
into a police car as my sister
waved from the ambulance.

Monkton 5:30

I was lost, aided by a clerk in a worn storefront.
I was driving past identical houses
swept by yards of blue snow,
each yellow window with a featureless figure.

How could I remember which way I turned?
I parked at a junction.
If we are duplicates,
why pour myself into another vacuum?

Granite Sill, Fourth Floor

In an attic workshop I assembled Tiffany lamps badly,
holding my uneven seams up to the window
then staring at the street below: a man spilling mustard
on his dress pants, a bus wheezing
in front of Caldor's, and pigeons carted by air.
Lead trickled over my knuckles
as I soldered plaques of colored glass.

I thought I would never be alive,
the most I could hope for would be the walk
into the morning-glazed building,
following the trail of someone's perfume in the
stairwell.

Late Afternoon

My mother dragged me to the window
to watch my father, drunk, leaving the widow's car.

You see what he does.

The widow and her two young daughters
had been in a fire. The widow had a red ring
and a blue ring on her long fingers grazing my cheek.

The younger would show me her puckered skin
if I took off my clothes and danced.

Annex

My great-grandfather and great uncle
inhabited an outbuilding.
At one end, two iron cots.
At the other, a woodstove,
an oilcloth-covered table,
a bowl of molasses kisses
wrapped in twists
of yellow waxed paper.

My great uncle never strayed beyond the woodshed
but my great-grandfather had been a carpenter in
town.

My grandmother made their dinner and supper
and pulled identical work clothes in enormous sheets
from the wringer washer.

Western Front

Standing way behind
the front lines, my father
was drinking scotch
with a couple of soldiers.
The tall one from another company
traded scotch for German souvenirs.
The first time it ate a hole
in my father's canteen
but eventually, he got a plastic one.
The guy in the middle,
his knees sagging, fell
and his head cracked
into the hard-packed dirt,
shot in the neck.

My father said,
I never expected to live.
I paddled across the river.
I could see a few Germans
but not the tunnels under the houses.

When the planes flew
into the Twin Towers
he catapulted back
nearly sixty years and woke
with his hands on a boiling kettle.

I was back at war,
I could smell the camps.

With a circle of chin
stitched like a baseball,
he limps with his bandaged hands before him.
They gave me all-new blood
but I'm still tired.

Drugged, he vacations in a past
strewn with happiness,
his ebullient hospital gown
swarming over the bed.

Cold War

My father made a still
next to our air-raid shelter.
The men passed the jug around,
choking and weeping,
their faces blistering,
saying *this is good.*

Then the rare great aunts arrived
in identical floral bosoms.
Each mashed my face in her cleavage
and fluffed my hair with embroidered handkerchiefs.

The men wiped their bright lips on their arms
in girlish embarrassment, jostling the cigarette packs
rolled in the sleeves of their tee shirts.

Belfast

After "Belfast," a documentary by
Frederick Wiseman

Rain hits the wind chimes; a slight belling.
Deaf, the old man watches the lips of his nurse.
He wants something; he flails,
it sinks over him and he pushes it off.
The fish slide into the next bin
in the fish factory, and a worker adjusts the hair
net half over his beard. The worker and the nurse
have a daughter at the sheltered workshop
gluing dowels into blocks of wood. They are going
to forgive her father for what he did, and hope
his nurse whistles as he shuffles his walker forward
and cannot hear him.

First Period

Brave Mrs. Kenley turns her back on the first grade,
and like a grass fire, from raw blade to raw blade,
enmity spreads.

Mr. Hawkins twists paperclips
around his knuckles.

Mrs. Thompson and Mrs. Hall sit at their stern desks,
squinting at long absent children, shuddering
at the mirage of Theodore, his head clean and empty
as a silver pond. No cultivated seed grew in his acre,
no stray fact lodged between his teeth.
The void must be extracted,
that was the clock for Theodore.

Mrs. Thompson remembers him
without even the fondness
one feels for a good meal.

Coast

In the seaside town where we lived
I ran across mud flats at low tide
and walked stonebreakers to the endpoint.

I watched horseshoe crabs mate,
one armor-plated creature on another.

My sixth-grade teacher
picked me off the floor as he danced
and swung me in a circle as I drooled.

Musical Figures 2

1. Dead cluster flies under rubber-soled shoes
2. The electric fan and the pause at the end of its oscillation
3. A cricket under the cold stove
4. Ice stirred in a pitcher
5. Newspapers twisted into wands for the fire
6. The thumping of wood stacked
7. The TV warming up
8. Boots tapping on icy puddles
9. The aluminum legs of the chair dragged across the floor
10. The cushion in the chair relenting

Potatoes

I am roasting a chicken
and arguing. Change appears
slowly, the slow browning in the oven,
my thickened waist bulging in my tee shirt.
Am I mistaking
this spasm of anger for future pattern?

A nice roaring I make
perusing the funnels and torrents of rage.

How grateful I was
for that one afternoon I could see something;
not a blight moving across the floor, one
strong light over the kitchen sink,
one garden of mint & pennyroyal waving

an ocean where I am less tried.

Staging

After "Preparation" by Czeslaw Milosz

As soon as I have finished preparing,
I will be able to tell the truth.
It will include the mountains and their absence
in the lives of certain troubled peoples.
I can already say the painted things,
the bits of work on the stage,
see, I can make the smoke appear
after the cannons have fired.
I am certain permission is about to go through.
I have passed the exams.
In view of my history,
they may feel I've cheated.

Perhaps.

Oak

My mother made me take a pill
before they carried me to the dentist.

It's to calm you, she said, and I ran.

His hand on the tree trunk,
I could see my father through the leaves
as I swung up another level.

I was shamefully old, eleven,
crouching in the branches,
each foot besieged.

First Confession

Stephen ground my face in the snowbank
and ran to his mother's house.
Martin smelled like cow shit
and held my hand in third grade.
My best friend held a velvet postcard
of the Virgin Mary glowing in the dark.

I loved her and wanted to marry her
though she committed mortal sins.

We wanted God to keep us forever
riding our bikes over the iron bridge,
waving to our distant parents.

Hearth

The chair by the fire
the fire unlit
the window spider-tracked
the rug hummocked

I begin, my awkward elbows braced,
pang-sorted, my natural stall
to lean into silence

a cough and a hope dangling

and dawn and ending,
slippers and shoes
by the fender.

Chimera

I was busy fleeing my birth;
in a movie I would have shouted
don't go by yourself
and I didn't,
the one that stayed twisted
to watch me look back —
a phantom does the suffering.

I couldn't find myself for years:
my sister's hands taped to my wrists,
my mother's eyes above and below.

The Balkans

My mother pounded on the back of my older sister
pushing her down the front steps
and threw her mascara after her,
my sister waiting until evening
when my father brought her back in the house.

My mother curled into the couch.
The doctor told me to rest.

Then work, food and the brown couch
we slept on in the vastness of the living room
vanished.

We were divided by my younger sister's birth;
my brother to the air force.

In the next place we lived
she tied the baby to a chair
and threw her,
once, against the wall.

I can't remember what?
A medical procedure
my mother performed
on my younger sister.
I remember my sister screaming.
It makes my shoulders roil even now.

Sometimes at night I think I hear someone crying
but it's the glue of everyday life,
the dog snoring, the refrigerator churning.

My younger sister lived at home until she was thirty,
sidling between adolescence and old age.
She and my mother watched TV, dozed and
sickened. My mother grew thin, my sister fat,
and my father circled outside them, raging
I've given them everything.

Events, like place,
are a side effect of time.

When he was seventeen and
I was seven, my brother
offered me twenty dollars
to touch my crotch.
He pleaded,
hand under his suit pants.
When I was younger
he said *mom said to do this*

and time left him forever seventeen.

Wearing a flannel nightgown,
my older sister tripped over a cord.

My father ripped the cord out,
beating channels through her gown.
My mother said
look what you've done
but she was smiling
nervously, rage was not a consolation.

Guilt ate every one of us.

Apple Tree

I can't get her to stop peeing her pants,
said my mother.
Well, said my grandmother,
if she wants to act like a baby,
treat her like a baby.

They pinned a towel at my hips
and it sagged between my legs.

Spackled into a tree with my cousins,
as one they bent their heads
to the side and tsked, tsked.

City Bus

My fever hovered over
long evenings in the hospital
and the nurse said
you're going to be here forever

in clean linen sheets but gasping
with my books beside me but silenced
unlike the boy in the next bed over
whose brain was erupting,
who cried when they moved him.

Released and returned to school
I got on the wrong bus
the lip of the door sealing
and the lurch forward
afraid the right bus would never come.

Furious rounds I traveled
to streets I didn't know,
clasped in my waiting.

Laces

My teacher said I'd better shape up
or I'd be left behind
but it was not until second grade
I was told to gather my pencil box
and move back. As the teacher pointed out,
only one child couldn't tie her shoes.

It was years before my teachers wrote
she could do better.

Dining Out

When my father climbs out of the restaurant, he's ten
years older.

His hands mottle in the sun when he resurfaces.
Scared, he returns for a drink.

He dives back to his table
and his war buddies are there.
When he leaves, the sidewalk is being bombed.
He falls to the ground, tastes cement dust.

He rejoins his buddies, laughing.
The war drops him behind enemy lines,
his outstretched hand reaching towards us.

Forty or fifty years pass, he can't remember.
He leaves the restaurant an old man
trying to cross the street to his front porch,
lilacs in bloom and ivy climbing the chimney.

Spider

1.
When I was a boy
I was thrown so hard
the chair broke under me,
my father said,
and they dangled a spider in my hair.

His mother ironed a sharp 'V'
on the forearm of her daughter.

My aunt circled the common room
of the state hospital all through my childhood,
wearing plaid slippers and a blue housedress,
the scar nudging her sleeve.

2.
My mother never let us stay with my father's parents.
Never, she said, her hands buried in dishwater.

Parceled out, I rode in the front seat
between my shrunken grandmother shaking
and my grandfather blinking at the dashboard.

I watched the speedometer creep into the red,
then, a silent supper and
I was ushered into bed,
my grandmother singing behind me.

Linseed Oil

My mother is painting swans
on a canvas propped by the TV,
resuming the life abandoned in eighth grade.

She drew girls in diaphanous pants
in the margins of her notebook
and was banned
from the homes of certain farmers.

Forty, she graduates high school
and learns to drive. My father
builds a fire in the fireplace
if you dress like that
they'll think you're crazy.

Poem for a War Zone

I rub my thumb over the letters
carved almost before his life began.

Rising, I clasp your hand.
What of us can be resurrected?

We created the kingdom of his childhood
and never found him again.

We must have driven past him
with nothing in our hands
but what had already fallen.

Musical Figures 3

1. A paintbrush slapping against baseboards
2. Chicken frying
3. A rusted swing set on a windy day
4. The punch of a ball kicked across the playground
5. A janitor pushing a broom in an empty auditorium
6. Frogs fleeing the banks of the pond
7. A stick in the spokes of a bicycle wheel
8. A propane torch bearing down on cold metal

My Formative Years

Not long ago I felt like green apples:
young but sour, then like potatoes
squat in the cushioning dark.

Also, as though I were twenty-five cents,
rolling in a small circumference.

My skin ignited in air.

How could I know
how insufficient I was
for this poisoned world?

Factory Floor

When I was mired
I wanted someone
with genial wings
to ease me to a paradise.

Over time I recognized
my limited incandescence
and shunted my alien face,
the obverse of pity,
past the handsome world.

I could not be reconciled
to want and to hate.
I wedged myself
in work, forcing my eyes
to only the strata before me,
to only what can be promised,
which is nothing.

The Library

My mother took me.
I looked at the stacks of books,
smelled mildew in dim corners.
I imagined something different
and we couldn't keep them

but my mother didn't drive then;
could my aunt have taken us?
Her husband rarely let her out of the house,
she had no indoor plumbing,
would she have had a car?

Could my father have taken us?
He said my mother taught him to read
but I never saw him hold a book.

Could our neighbor have taken us,
a war bride with an indifferent grasp of English?

Holiday

My father, in a clean T-shirt, is holding a knife
above the Thanksgiving turkey, but he is looking
at my mother as she stares at a chipped bowl
of peas and plucks loose threads from her sleeve,
the scythe and anchor of us.

Machinist

1.
My father thought the lamp was swaying
but it was the ladder. The pipe wrench
fell after, crumpling his skull.

His hands dangled outside the hospital sheets.
He was stapled to machines,
his head swaddled, like the others
who looked like they had lain there
since some prehistoric war,
a blink and a groan
the entire remnant of their memory.

When he woke he wanted a drink
but shrugged his shoulders in resignation
to the clump of doctors.

Since he was there,
could they repair his arthritis?
Perhaps some of them
didn't have enough to do.

His feet surer than his memory,
he went home after a month of idling,
his conversation narrowed
to the brief spasms that made his arms shake.

2.
My father carried home machines
to salvage: half a generator
under the dining room table,
a failed air conditioner in the bedroom.

Outside, a small stack of cars.
Hold the light up
my father said and I shined it on the carburetor.
He took out some parts.
Cars were changing
and he couldn't remember.

He knows, said my brother
more than any two mechanics.

It was raining and he couldn't make it run.

His father had been a blacksmith
for the railroad, knocking skeins
of cars together in the switchyard,
the chain of commotion his.

Hannibal Crosses the Alps

My mother raises the broom
over my brother and sister engaged
in their libretto of injury and revenge,
the broom a muffled snare.

She sweeps them into separate corners.
I never wanted you, I never wanted any of you.

They know this and battle
for a province they can win.

Summer

My aunt was wearing a sleeveless shirt,
the smell of sweat mixing with the smell of
strawberries
in her small kitchen.
We sat around the silver-flecked table.
I scratched the edges of congealed coffee rings.

The sun dazzled the ashtray.
Through curls of cigarette smoke
cream streamed in our bowls.

Ash Brook

I walked from my grandparents'
to the brook with my father.
I found a rock to sit on
and he gave me a fishing pole.
Shh, he said as I splashed,
and put down his pole.

He put his hand on my back
and pointed to fish darting under rocks
they'll bite when it's quiet
and walked upstream from me.

That winter the snow froze to a hard crust
and my sister and I ice-skated
from the crest to the brook
heaving clouds of steam
from its moving pools.

Pembroke Lane

We moved to a cabin skirting a wealthy suburb.

We kept milk for the baby
in a picnic cooler.
We dug dandelion greens
from the lawn in the yawning fall
and an uncle brought eggs.

My father found work.
My mother drank martinis
in the early dark of winter.

Dressed in the cast-off clothes
of my classmates,
I scratched and slapped as
they teased me,
pinned and dangling
from an endless arm.

Space Program

Marilyn Monroe dies the year we shuffle
into the gym to watch John Glenn in his slow orbit
across the monumental sky.

Mrs. Tofani, the fourth-grade teacher,
exhorts us to remember this day
and I remember Martin threw a rock
ushering a geyser of blood from Danny's head
and Mrs. Tofani pressing paper towels on him,
as though she was forcing him into the ground.

At night I thought of Mrs. Tofani
helping me into my ship or suit
as I lay sweating in my bed.

My Grandmother's Rug

I spent hours brushing my hair,
watching particles of dust
drift in a drum of sun.

The pediatrician gave me something
and I thrummed the TV tray,
twitched until my shoulder
pulled backward to my heels.

I lay on the braided rug,
staring at its tufts of yellow and brown,
tracing the grit in its creases,
my hand wired in my furls of hair
as my father rubbed my back.

At Rest

My father lowered his arm
slowly resting his knuckles
against my mother's cheek
until it was evening of the next day.

Prescient

My mother murmured into the phone
she knew everything
but couldn't go to the pharmacy
because the pharmacist read her mind.

Her doctor sent her to the hospital.
We visited her in the atrium
and ate on linen tablecloths.

Reason took center stage for a moment.
She saw us as though standing on us,
eyes stuffed with glass.

Categories

My father's sputtering conversation clapped in time
to ice knocking in his drink.

Look at that, my mother says
to atrocity and the price of bacon,
catastrophes of equal measure.
She paints fairies on teacups
and walks the street
handing out dollar bills.

My mother sorts her collection
of sugar packets and plastic bags.

All the kids have sided with their father.
The police, the pastor, none
rescue her despite her frequent calls.

His physical therapist, the receptionist, none
save him though my mother thinks each
his secret lover.

And the social workers
bumping against each other
on the narrow couch
have neither love nor cure.

She moves to the microwave —
the meals she made, the loads of laundry.
She cuts one leg off his dress pants.
She mails each child an empty box.

*Don't you believe people can do anything
if they try,* asked my sister.

I shook my head,
my parents were an argument emptied
of everything but motion.

My father sawed her paintings in half,
she threw his seizure medication into the snow,
the green and blue traces like lively worms.

After we divided them,
after my mother's stroke,
I would hang jewelry on her
when my father came to visit.

My father, marooned in the place
he wanted, cries over the phone
I miss her so much.
He sends her a letter.
You don't have any friends now, do you?

Musical Figures 4

1. The sigh when hands release the steering wheel
2. Dirt sifting onto cement steps
3. A hand tapping on asphalt shingles, waiting for the door to open
4. Crying in a hallway
5. A wrench falling to the floor, gloves following
6. A coffee cup sloshing
7. A belt sliding through loops
8. Sticks on an oil drum

Dream

We wandered through my grandfather's house
sorting plates and twigs
and throwing pebbles out the window.
In the yard, swifts tangled in our hair
and we couldn't find our way back.

We met two women coming back from a wedding,
one in a beaded vest. They gave us a glass of wine
and for years we quarreled about recipes.

We followed the wide path out of town
and found our own house blackened.

In a clearing between two birches
were our broken pots and mildewed clothes
and I wept for the things grown old without me.

Road Trip

We slept by the highway in West Virginia.
I don't remember how we made it that far.

By morning the gullies of the sleeping bag were filled
with snow.
In the few houses strewn beneath the overpass
we could smell cornbread frying and hear dogs.
Because his parents were wealthy, he was supposed to
bring money.
He unrolled a candy bar and a quarter,
his broad shoulders shaking as he wept.

We turned back, a long way from New Jersey.

I knew someone in the splatter of houses would take us
in,
and I would have my hand on him
to show he was meek, and slowly nod
to show I was wise.

A Tragedy in Three Acts

1.
I was driving past Wal-Mart
when the transmission fell out of my car.

2.
It reminded me of bumping my suitcase
up the steps of the Greyhound
when the cover sprang open,
festooning the passengers with my underwear.

3.
At school, we played polio victim.
The smallest, I was daily lugged
by grieving classmates
from tarmac to apple tree
where a miracle occurred because
I didn't want to be the main corpse.

Artemisia

In her Southwestern window
my grandmother dressed, the bedroom
wintry, mint walls, silver earrings
and photographs, the buttressed
undergarments, her cleavage splashed
with something besides grandchildren,
we were weaving ourselves
into the runners on the dresser, and the gold coming
in the sunset, and we could not be removed.

When my mother died
I saw my grandmother waking
from her casket at my footboard,
her hand tugging at my quilt.

North Bradford

My grandparents were a clock
peeling the new
from everything age adorns,
the Sunday table set with ruby glasses
and lipstick-colored blossoms pricking the air
near the hutch of souvenir plates.

My grandfather said
madam will have her roast chicken
and shrugged; the silo full,
wheat surging through the weeds.

The Fifth Winter of My Grandmother

Her father, drunk, tied her to a sled
and walked quietly through the snow
to leave her with a distant relative,
the sawing of the runners,
the creak of the crossbar as he pulled,
an owl above the now clear,
now distant figure of her father
as snow shifted around him.

Her father didn't die, not then,
but disappeared in the same woods.

It was her mother she searched for,
her mother who had plucked
the oldest and the youngest to leave
and reset the table for four,
a blue water pitcher, roast potatoes, salt pork.

No matter how many times
my grandmother cooks the same meal,
they never take her back.

My Mother at Six

She's playing school
with a stony desk
giving lessons but not orating
to the trees as she did later

wandering then with a biscuit in hand
tutoring the fears of her younger brother.

Some landscape must ease
the survey of rubble and empty hand.

Sunday Visit

I wonder why the sum
of human experience
is a scrap of cloth
revealing and swathing
our failures.

We don't need to talk about philosophy,
the gravel slick as we stand in the driveway,
rain on the steadfast house
no one can bear to enter.

Statues

Her care dwindled to me, and
the cache of our small history.
This is what she drew in the sand,
this is all she had to say
in her final night.

This is all I could know,
this is the only treatment
for the ways we infected
each other, here is a yellow
thumbnail much pried from the door.

Memorial

My hair turns white
and my teeth gray,
this is the album of the forgotten:
the lilac in your hair and
the suitcase carried among buses and trains,
the station you never left, collapsed on the dry floor.
Here is the chorus erasing your last words
in the susurration of consolation.

Another Rider

What I was doing on the train was walking
to the dining car for chicken salad and a glass of white
wine,
carrying the travels of Admiral Peary, sighing as I do
at the click of cars through the mountain pass and
losing
my breath for the bridge — matchsticks balanced over a
gorge.
My ignorance sneaks in front of me, the trees
unnamable
and a churning backyard fight passed; a witness
without voice.

My father said once he was sorry for what happened in
. . . and he paused.
Was it me he was talking to or another ghost in his ear?
His conversations chased a fortune on the horizon
while his voice circled a shrug.
I was his Cassandra, finishing my description while he
wove an opposing tale from the news, looking for the
right story with his name chalked beside it — an
incantation before he slept.

Bench

I hear a man pounding nails into wood,
how good to be making something
that's not hammering into the living
but the cask left over,
sealing the final form.

For the First Attempt

Dark head propped on white pillows,
knees clapped together under white sheets,
she lists slowly to the wall
and counts tiles,
now everything must be rebuilt.

She turns back and lies
to the awkward doctor
standing by the bed rails,
his ears plugged into a song about nothing.

What Winter

Dark in the early morning
and traffic trolling past my driveway.

I don't know what winter plants the best spring.
I run my hands over the spines of books
for the consolation of order.

The monotony we bring with us,
fragments of the buried speech of our parents,
and our inevitable reversion.

Beholder

The cherry tree bends
not from its fruit
but cold. Cold
has more desire
than tree or beholder
to make a pleasing form.

I decided to stand
under what shelter
might be offered by the tree
and let all topical routine
submerge under the actual sap
that gilds fruit and dream alike.

I want an orange tree
to blossom in my yard with a man wearing a kilt
dancing beneath while a deer
with heavy antlers watches and fruit encloses
man, deer and shining tree.

My authority rests in the chair I sit in,
its rails and fabric,
and in the bitter seeds
I have found on my plate.

Speech

I have other stories, who doesn't,
and what to say of them and when,
to massage the stiffness of my old dreams.
I want to do for myself
what was started by others, to prune.

This is all I will say for now
as I close the pages and feel the wine
and afternoon and promises.

Musical Figures 5

1. Reading in an empty room
2. Blinds pulled up
3. Asking, where are you?
4. Spaghetti sauce cooking on the back of the stove
5. Someone sick, coughing in bed
6. Walking across carpet, walking across hardwood
7. Eyeglasses falling on the bedside table
8. Clothes on hangers, moving on the rod in the closet
9. Syllables in sleep
10. Panoply and a counter of scarves in a discount store

Acknowledgments

Poems from this collection will appear or have appeared in:

Agni Online — "Dream"
Anomaly Literary Journal — "Lost Ticket"
Antigonish — "A Tragedy in Three Acts & Dining Out"
Chaffin Journal — "Belfast"
Elixir — "Tic"
English Journal — "Cold War"
Gyroscope — "Another Rider"
Inch — "The Sale, Chimera" (as "Our Common History")
Labor: Studies in Working-Class History — "Annex & Granite Sill" (Spring 23)
Mom Egg — "Eulogy"
Mudlark — "Staging" (as "After Milosz"), "North Bradford" (as "Unclaimed Territories")
Panoply — "43 Howland Street"
Pedestal — "My Formative Years"
Ploughshares — "Beholder"
Plume — "Monkton 5:30" (forthcoming)
Poet-Lore — "The Fifth Winter of My Grandmother" (& reprinted in *Mountain Troubadour*)
Raritan — "Musical Figures 4", "Musical Figures 5", "Oak", "Laces" (as "Second Grade")
Sinister Wisdom — "The Balkans", "First Confession" (also in *Roads Taken Anthology*), "Prescient"
Tilde~ — "Hearth"
Verse-Virtual — "For the First Attempt", "Road Trip", "Sunday", "Devon"; "City Bus", "Poem for a War Zone"

Thanks to: Ann Turkle, Dawnine Spivack, Eva Zimet, Grace Johnstone, Joan Aleshire, Marjorie Ryerson, Martha Zweig, Merry Gangemi, Scudder Parker, Vermont Community Foundation, and Vermont Studio Center.

And especially thanks to my wife, Jackie Johnson.

About the Author

Samn Stockwell has published in *Agni, North American Review*, and *The New Yorker*, among others. *Musical Figures* is her third book of poetry. Her two previous books, *Theater of Animals* and *Recital*, won the National Poetry Series (USA) and the Editor's Prize at Elixir, respectively. Recent poems are in *On the Seawall* & *Sugar House Review* and are forthcoming in *Ploughshares*, among others.

About the Publisher

Thirty West Publishing House
Handmade Chapbooks (and more) since 2015
www.thirtywestph.com / thirtywestph@gmail.com
You should follow us! Consider being a patron?
@thirtywestph